T0348912

Carolyn Forster is a best-selling quilting author, with over 150,000 books sold worldwide. She started making quilts when she was a teenager, and her passion for patchwork and quilting led her to study Textiles at Bath Spa University, UK. Since then, she has taught patchwork and quilting both in the UK and the USA and has had her quilts featured in a number of books and magazines, including *Today's Quilter* and French magazine *Magic Patch*. Carolyn lives in Tunbridge Wells, UK.

www.carolynforster.co.uk

 @quiltingonthego

Other books in this series:

The original best-selling Twenty to Make *series has sold over 2 million copies worldwide! Each book in this new series is published in hardback pocket-size format, making them perfect little gifts.*

9781782219675

9781782219811

9781800920989

9781800921764

9781800922044

9781782219767

9781800920873

9781800921399

9781800921009

9781800921603

9781800921467

9781800922044

ALL-NEW

20

TO MAKE

ONE-PATCH QUILTS

Carolyn Forster

SEARCH PRESS

DEDICATION

For those who like to use up all of their fabric.

This edition first published in 2025
This book uses material previously published in *20 to Stitch One-Patch Quilts*, 2017

Search Press Limited
Wellwood, North Farm Road,
Tunbridge Wells, Kent TN2 3DR

ISBN: 978-1-80092-258-7
ebook ISBN: 978-1-80093-257-9

Publishers' note
The Publishers and author can accept no responsibility for any consequences
arising from the information, advice or instructions given in this publication.

Readers are permitted to reproduce any of the items in this book for their personal
use, or for the purposes of selling for charity, free of charge and without the prior
permission of the Publishers. Any use of the items for commercial or machine
learning purposes is not permitted without the prior permission of the Publishers.

Suppliers
For information regarding the materials and equipment mentioned in this book,
please visit the Search Press website: www.searchpress.com

Bookmarked Hub
Extra copies of the templates are available to download free from the
Bookmarked Hub. Search for this book by title or ISBN: the files can be found
under 'Book Extras'. Membership of the Bookmarked online community is free:
www.bookmarkedhub.com

About the author
Find out more about Carolyn and discover more of her work:
• on her website: www.carolynforster.co.uk
• on Instagram: @quiltingonthego

MIX
Paper | Supporting
responsible forestry
FSC® C136333
www.fsc.org

INTRODUCTION

Patchwork quilts sewn from just one pattern piece can offer endless satisfaction from a design point of view, as well as being easy to cut and sew. To start with, there is the great ease of only ever having to cut one shape out.

The 20 blocks in this book are each made with just one patch. The designs they produce are often referred to as tessellating patterns, as the shapes connect to each other with no gaps in between.

One-patch quilts are great for the novice as well as the experienced sewer. One simple shape, such as a square, can simply be sewn as a 'happy scrappy' quilt, where the positioning of fabrics is random and the same fabric is used more than once. A more complicated shape such as the jewel, for example, is slightly more tricky to sew, but a whole range of design possibilities exist, all depending on your fabric selection.

One-patch quilts can also be sewn as charm quilts; this is when each piece of the quilt is stitched from a different piece of fabric. These quilts are often created over a long period of time while the fabrics are being collected. To speed up the process, people often exchange fabrics with fellow quilters or family members. Fabrics from old clothes can be used, as well as pieces swapped with friends and family, making them into a memory quilt.

One of the first documented single-patch quilts was a hexagon quilt in *Godey's Lady's Book*, published in 1835. This patch is still a favourite, but there are many others that offer design versatility. You will see in the following pages some of the ideas that these quilts can inspire. Each project includes the template at actual size and one or two ideas for putting your shapes together (although there are many more than we have space for!).

The patches in the book come roughly in order of stitching difficulty, but don't let that influence your choice of patch – let your imagination and your fabrics take the lead. Make your patchwork as large or as small as time and fabrics allow, and refer to the stitching know-how information on pages 6–13 for basic guidelines on joining, quilting and finishing.

Finally, included on pages 60–64, is a full-size quilt project made up using a combination of one-patch quilt blocks. Enjoy mixing and matching the 20 blocks to create your own fabulous designs.

TOOLS AND MATERIALS

FABRIC

Cotton dress-weight fabrics are the easiest to stitch with if you are just starting out. Scraps of old clothes will hold personal memories and are fun to include and use. Make sure you choose areas of fabric that are not worn out. Any fabric you use should be clean and pressed flat.

THREAD

Stitch with a good-quality sewing thread using a colour that tones with your fabrics.

TOOLS

SCISSORS

Paper-cutting scissors are necessary for cutting templates, card and plastic. These should be comfortable to handle with a sharp blade.

Most sewists will have separate scissors for fabric: use a pair that are not too big for your hand and that you feel in control of. My favourite scissors for cutting patches are ones with a slightly serrated edge. These seem to grip the fabric as you cut and allow for nice precise work.

RULERS & TOOLS

Your basic rotary cutter rulers are all useful for marking a ¼in (5mm) seam allowance (SA) when needed, especially the smaller sizes as they are easier to handle.

PENS AND PENCILS

A propelling pencil designed for fabric is a good choice as it will always be sharp. Use a fine permanent marker pen for drawing onto template plastic, so the ink does not transfer to the fabric.

ROTARY CUTTER

Like a pizza wheel, a rotary cutter cuts through up to about eight layers of fabric at a time. Keep the blade sharp and free of nicks.

SELF-HEALING CUTTING MAT

This purpose-made mat is available from craft and patchwork stores and is used in conjunction with a rotary cutter and rotary-cutting rulers or templates for cutting fabric. It is marked into a grid that you can use to help you measure and cut the fabric in straight lines. Buy the largest size you can afford so you will not have to fold your fabric so much.

THIMBLE

Thimbles can protect your fingers during the stitching process but they may take a bit of getting used to. I like to wear a dimpled metal thimble on my middle finger that pushes the needle, and a thimble with a ridge on the index finger of my other hand. This protects my finger as I make the stitches (see page 11).

PINS AND NEEDLES

I find either short appliqué pins or fine patchwork pins best for pinning patches together when sewing. Either way, the finer the pin, the better the job it will do for you.

I use a sharps no. 10 needle for hand piecing, but personal preferences vary, so use what you are comfortable with – just make sure you can thread it easily and that it gives you the results you are looking for. Never be afraid to experiment with a new needle type.

USING THE TEMPLATES

You can use the template shapes in this book as they are, or increase or reduce the size on a photocopier, but the important thing is to keep the seam allowance (SA) at ¼in (5mm).

The most important things to note are:

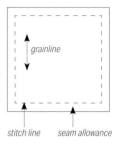

stitch line   seam allowance

• All the templates include the grainline, a ¼in (5mm) SA and also show the stitch line (see example, right). If you want a template without a SA, draw along the inner dashed line (the stitch line) of the template diagram.

• If you are hand sewing and want to draw in the stitch line, draw around a template cut to the size of the stitch line; then, before cutting out the fabric, add on an additional ¼in (5mm) SA all around, by eye, giving you the full size.

• If you are confident sewing without the marked stitch line, simply draw and cut out the patches at the SA line, and then sew them together using your presser foot width to guide you as to the SA.

Make your templates from firm card or template plastic. Template plastic is easy to cut with scissors and very durable. Use a fine-line permanent marker pen to label the template and note any stitching lines. Clear template plastic acts as a great window template if you want to use a certain motif from a fabric, as you can see through it to position it correctly. If you are repeating a motif for fussy cutting you can add balance points so that you always match the motif accordingly. If you are using card as your template, photocopy the template and then stick it to the card. Cut out along the printed line. A card template is fine, but will not be as accurate if you use it repeatedly, as the edges become soft after a while.

If you have cut your fabric to include the SA, but need to mark a stitching line, use a small rotary cutting ruler, and line the ¼in (5mm) line up to the raw edge. Mark your sewing line using the edge of the ruler, making either a solid line or dashes.

If you have drawn the stitching line onto your fabric, you can always add the SA as you cut, judging it by eye. There is no need to measure precisely, as it will be your sewing line that you pin along, using this for accuracy, not the cut line.

DIE-CUTTING MACHINES

Lots of the one-patch designs in the book are popular shapes that many die-cutting machine companies produce. This is a great way to cut lots of patches accurately that include the SA. If you are thinking of using English Paper Piecing (EPP), also consider buying pre-cut papers, which come in lots of different sizes and multiple quantity packets.

DESIGN OPTIONS

There are so many ways to arrange these tessellating shapes that it would be almost impossible to describe them all.

Doodle on paper or print off downloadable grids from the internet to experiment with what is possible. Colour these in using a pencil or use coloured pens, depending on your working preference, so that you can see the patterns clearly, and you will begin to get an idea of the wide range of options that exist before you begin to stitch.

There are numerous variations for each of the templates in this book so, although there are just twenty shapes to start you off, there are so many more different quilt variations you could sew.

Bear in mind the scale and proportion of the design on the fabrics, too. If you have a large-scale print, then you might want to show this off with a larger template. If you like working with smaller patches, consider working on a smaller project such as a mini-quilt or a pillow cover.

One great use of the blocks is to create a selection of one-patch designs, then sew them all together with sashing – sampler-style – into one big quilt (see the Quilt project on pages 60–64).

HOW MUCH FABRIC WILL I NEED?

One-patch designs lend themselves to scrappy-style quilts or charm quilts. Quilt instructions for such designs do not usually come with fabric quantity guidelines. With the exception of the quilt project on page 60, because I am providing ideas for quilts in this book, rather than instructions on making specific quilts, there are no fabric quantities given, as there are too many variables, for example: how big is my template? And how big do I want my finished quilt to be?

Some guidelines will help you to calculate how much fabric you need for a particular project. The way I work is as follows:

1 Find out how many templates you can cut from a fat quarter of fabric. Next, count how many templates fit across the width and then the length of the quilt. Multiply these together for the total number.

2 Divide this total number by the number of templates in a fat quarter. This number rounded up to a whole number will be the number of fat quarters you need.

This is just one way of working, so feel free to adapt it to your own methods.

STITCHING THE PATCHES

USING A SEWING MACHINE

All the patches in the book can be sewn on a machine (with the exception of the clam shell on page 50), but you will need to pay special attention to stitching the set-in pieces or curved pieces. These patches do not need a sewing line, as you will be guided by the ¼in (5mm) piecing foot on the sewing machine; cut them with the SA included.

When sewing the patches on the machine, you will be sewing through the seam allowance, unless you are setting pieces in. As you stitch through the seam allowance there is no need to secure the thread at the end of each seam. If you want the stitches to be more secure, then reduce your stitch length slightly to make a tighter seam.

If you are stitching multiple pieces, then you can 'chain piece' by feeding the next set of patches under the foot as the last ones come out at the back. This saves thread and time.

Most patchwork pieces can be sewn in straight lines, but some require you to sew around a corner. This is known as a set-in seam or a 'Y' seam. For this to happen smoothly, you need to stop stitching where the ¼in (5mm) seam allowances intersect on the first seam of the 'Y'. Stop at this point and leave a tail of thread about 1in (2.5cm) long. This seam is then pressed open, thus allowing you to sew in the third patchwork piece. By not sewing through the seam allowance here and pressing the seam open, you are able to stitch and pivot at the intersection, allowing you to sew round the corner smoothly and neatly.

SEWING BY HAND WITH RUNNING STITCH

If you have cut patches that include the SA, remember to mark in the stitching line if you don't feel experienced enough to judge by eye.

Thread the needle with toning thread no longer than the length of your arm. Start stitching with a knot and a backstitch and continue with a running stitch. Every inch (2.5cm) or so make a backstitch to help keep a good tension. When you reach the end of the sewing line, make two or three backstitches to finish. Cut the thread, leaving a tail about ½in (1.3cm) long.

Note:

Each design in the book is suitable for hand sewing, machine sewing and EPP. Some designs need to have set-in seams; these are the house (or prism), clam shell, hexagon and jewel (pages 26, 50, 52 and 54).

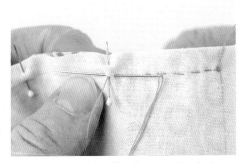

When hand piecing, start stitching with a knotted thread and a backstitch. Continue sewing with a running stitch, and add in a backstitch every inch (2.5cm) or so. This helps keep the stitches secure and prevents them gathering up.

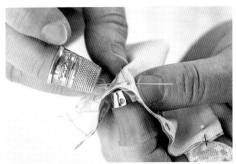

Thimbles will help protect your fingers when stitching. The dimpled metal thimble protects the finger that pushes the needle through and the ridged thimble on the index finger underneath helps form the stitches.

Patches with sewing line already drawn

As you have lines on each patch, it is these that you need to match up rather than the raw edges. Place two patches with right sides together with a pin going through the SA stopping point. Pin it into the other patch at the same point, and pin into the SA. Do the same at the other end, and when that is in place, use a couple of pins to match up the line between the two points, depending on the length of your seam.

Patches with no sewing line

These patches have the SA included, but no line to follow. If you are experienced then you will be able to stitch them together by eyeballing the sewing line. If you are not at that stage yet, then use a propelling pencil on the wrong side of the fabric to draw the line. Use a rotary cutting ruler or a Quilter's Quarter Marker™ to mark the line. You only need the line on the patch that will face you when you stitch.

Sewing by hand with papers

Also known as English Paper Piecing (EPP), this is perhaps the method most associated with one-patch or mosaic-style quilts. It is very precise and works well for some of the more intricate shapes that require set-in piecing. It is, however, more time-consuming due to the extra step of stitching or gluing the papers onto the fabric. Cut papers to the finished size of the patches. Fabric patches should be cut larger by ¼in (5mm) or ⅜in (1cm).

Place the paper on the wrong side of the fabric with a SA all round each side. Fold the fabric to the paper and tack/baste through all of the layers to keep the fabric in place, starting with a knot and finishing with a backstitch.

When the patches are ready, sew with right sides together using toning thread and an oversewing stitch to secure the edges together. When the design is complete, remove the tacking/basting from the patches and take the papers out.

COMPLETING A QUILT

Once the patchwork is complete, press it flat. Neaten up the edges by cutting them straight with scissors or a rotary cutter. If you want to keep any uneven edges that impart character to your quilt, you can appliqué the edges to a wide border on each side. This has the added advantage of making it larger without too much more work.

LAYERING AND TACKING/BASTING

Layer the patchwork onto wadding/batting and a backing fabric. Your wadding/batting and backing should be slightly larger than your patchwork top all around. Tack/baste the layers with tacking/basting stitches, spray baste glue or safety pins. The tacking/basting and pins will all be removed during the quilting process.

When basting or tacking the layers of a quilt together, remember that this is the only thing keeping everything in place as you quilt, so your pins or stitches need to be appropriately spaced. If you safety pin baste, the pins should be spaced a closed fist's width apart. If you thread baste, the grid of stitches needs to be about 7in (18cm) apart – or use your hand span as the gauge.

QUILTING

If you are stitching a quilt from one of the patches then a common way to quilt by hand would be outlining each piece ¼in (5mm) from the seam. A quicker way would be to hand-quilt a grid or an overall design on the patchwork. Diamonds and Amish waves are often seen as good overall designs and bring cohesion to a scrappy quilt.

If you want to machine quilt then, for me, making sure there are no ends to sew in is a prime concern! Again overall designs like lines (see top image, right) and grids (middle image, right) work well if you are using a walking foot. If you want to free motion quilt, then vermicelli (see bottom image, right), and variations on this are fun and work over a whole quilt. In this example, machine quilting and big-stitch hand quilting have been combined, and this contrast in the textures is often a nice addition.

Tying a quilt offers a speedy solution, as the quilt is tied at the tacking/basting stage, so you skip a whole stage of the process.

The quilt I made from some of the patterns in the book has been quilted in an all-over design to give continuity, on a long-arm quilting machine (see pages 60–64). This is a great option if you love the piecing but don't have the time for the quilting!

BINDING

Apply a sturdy binding to the quilt edges to finish it off. Cut the fabric strip 2½in (6.35cm) wide on the straight or bias. This continuous strip may need joins; make these on the bias to distribute the bulk of the join. Then fold the strip in half along its length, wrong sides together, and press flat. You can then bind the quilt using mitred corners or square corners. Sew by hand or machine stitch.

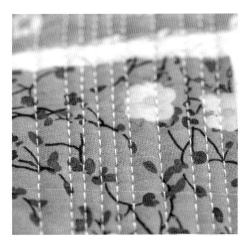

THE PROJECTS

SQUARE

The simplest and most common of shapes can be sewn into an infinite number of designs. Inspiration can be taken from cross stitch designs and pixelated images. To cut squares from fabric that include the seam allowance, any size you like, follow this simple formula: decide on the finished side size and add ¼in (5mm) for the seam allowance.

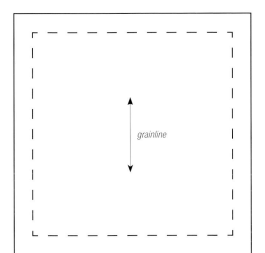

THE TEMPLATE

grainline

STITCHING

The squares can be stitched in rows (see Option 1) or in unit blocks (see Option 2), depending on the design and method of working. Choose whichever you prefer.

Option 1

Option 2

DESIGN IDEAS

Design idea 1 (as shown left)

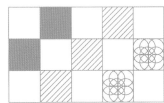

Design idea 2

HALF-SQUARE TRIANGLE

Triangles open up a whole new area of design ideas. Designs can be based on the play of light and dark within the square, or they can just be plain scrappy to use up what is at hand. To cut half-square triangles from fabric at any size you want (that includes the seam allowance), follow this simple formula: decide what length the finished side of the square will be and add a ⅞in (2.25cm) seam allowance. Then cut the square into two triangles.

THE TEMPLATE

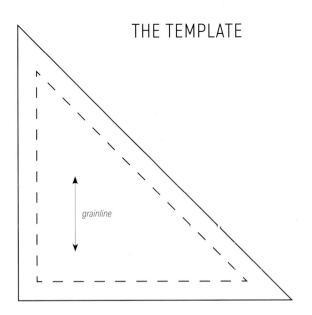

grainline

STITCHING

Sew the triangles together along the long bias edge to make squares first. Once these pieces are together, you can approach the stitching as you do with the squares on the previous page by working in rows or units.

DESIGN IDEAS

The design in the quilt shown opposite (Design 1) uses a simple, repeating pattern using contrasting lights and darks to emphasize the triangles.

Design idea 2

Design idea 3

Design idea 4

QUARTER-SQUARE TRIANGLE

Explore the design possibilities that a single unit of four triangles can make, or plan something larger depending on your time and fabric stash. To cut fabric quarter-square triangles any size you like, follow the simple formula: decide on the length of the longest side and cut squares of fabric adding a 1¼in (3cm) seam allowance to the square. Then cut the square into four triangles.

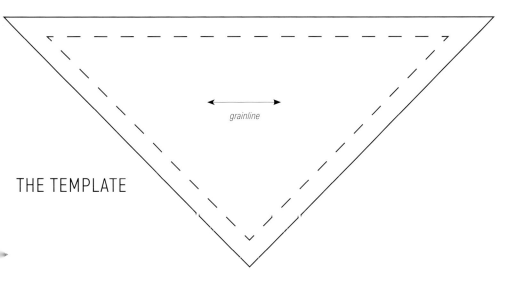

THE TEMPLATE

grainline

STITCHING

Sew the triangles into a strip by joining them along the bias edges (Option 1). Alternatively, stitch the triangles into squares first, then proceed to stitch these either into rows or to work in units (Option 2).

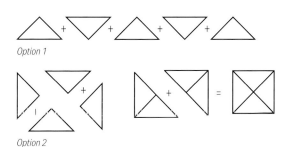

Option 1

Option 2

DESIGN IDEAS

The pattern in the quilt shown opposite (Design 1) shows a repeating stacked triangle effect.

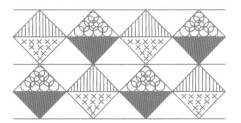

Design idea 2

Design idea 3

RECTANGLE TRIANGLE

These rectangle triangles offer many subtle and interesting designs, taking things one stage further than the basic triangle. Play with individual design units, or plan something stunning on a design wall.

THE TEMPLATE

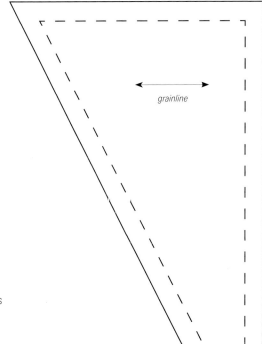

grainline

STITCHING

These can be approached in the same way as half-square triangles. Sew the pieces into rectangles first. Stitch the rectangles into rows or units to create your patchwork.

DESIGN IDEAS

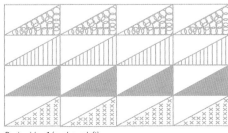

Design idea 1 (as shown left)

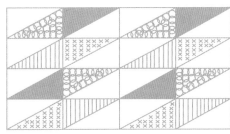

Design idea 2

RECTANGLE

Rectangles can be used quickly and easily for the simplest of brick-type quilt designs and played with endlessly to form secondary designs including pinwheels, stripes and medallions.

THE TEMPLATE

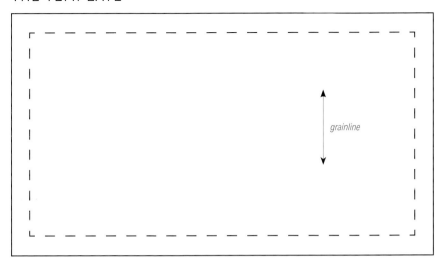

grainline

STITCHING

These can be approached in the same way as squares. Stitch into rows or units to create your patchwork.

Option 1

Option 2

DESIGN IDEAS

The pattern in this quilt follows Design idea 2, but with dark and light colours reversed for a different effect.

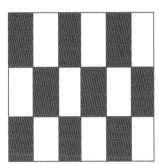

Design idea 1

Design idea 2

HOUSE OR PRISM

If you have not used this patch before, then you are in for a treat. Lined up in rows, it can look like streets of houses, yet transforms itself into a lovely abstract design unit when sewn in pinwheels of four.

THE TEMPLATE

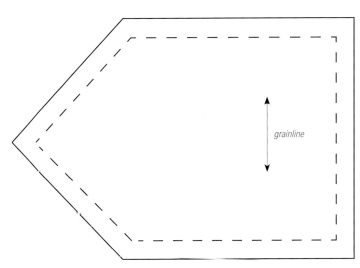

grainline

STITCHING

If you are working on the design in rows, like a street of houses, stitch the rows first. Then set the rows in to each other (see page 10). The remaining side of the row will be straight and you can sew this in a line.

Option 1

Option 2

Option 3

DESIGN IDEAS

The pattern in the quilt shown below and on
page 26 follows Design 1.

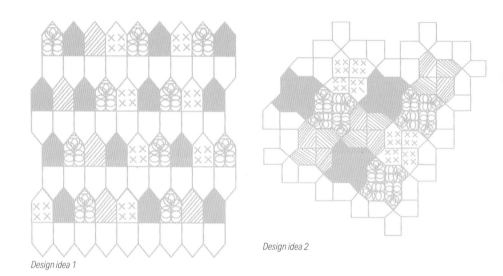

Design idea 1

Design idea 2

OFFSET SQUARE

This is a shape worth trying for the wonderful effects you can create with some very simple sewing. The shapes and designs created belie the simplicity of the stitching.

THE TEMPLATE

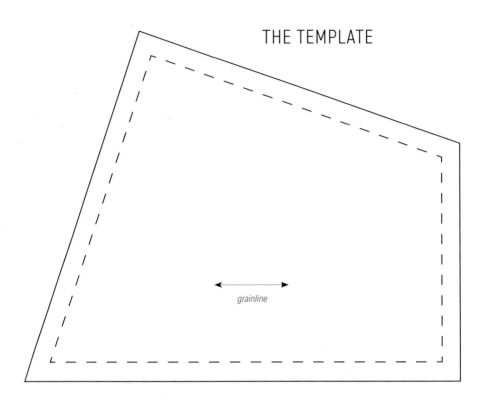

grainline

STITCHING

Stitch these together into their squares, then join the squares into rows. This makes for easy stitching of what could be viewed as a complicated design. Make sure you plan your fabric layout carefully before you start.

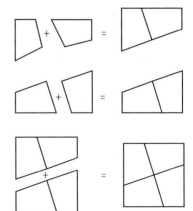

DESIGN IDEAS

The pattern in this quilt follows Design 2, creating an attractive windmill design.

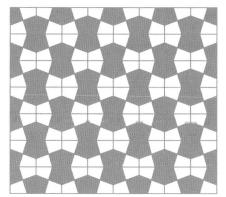

Design idea 1

Design idea 2

TILE OR DOUBLE PRISM

This patch makes a truly charming quilt and is great for using up fabric scraps. With some planning, you can create new shapes using some clever colour placement.

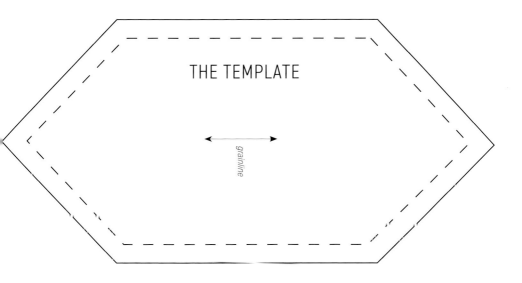

THE TEMPLATE

grainline

STITCHING

Stitch the patches together in rows, side by side, starting and stopping ¼in (5mm) from the raw edge. Then set these rows into each other, pivoting at each turn. It may seem fiddly to start with, but you will soon get the hang of it.

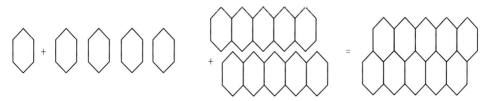

DESIGN IDEAS

The pattern in the quilt shown opposite (Design 1) shows a random design on a blue theme.

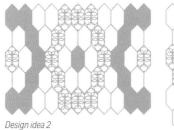

Design idea 2

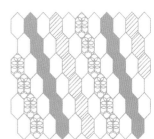

Design idea 3

45° DIAMOND

Lots of interesting patterns can be created with this simple diamond, but the stitching is usually very straightforward.

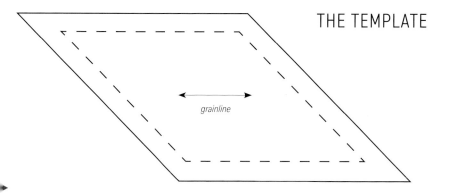

THE TEMPLATE

grainline

STITCHING

This patch is most easily stitched in straight lines of rows of patches.
Flip the shape over to create designs with more movement, such as
the zigzag in the quilt, left.

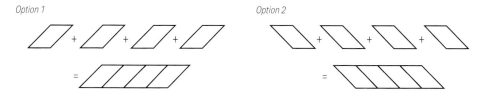

Option 1

Option 2

DESIGN IDEAS

The pattern in the quilt shown opposite (Design 1)
follows an attractive zigzag across the piece.

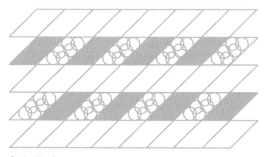

Design idea 2

Design idea 3

60° DIAMOND

At first glance this is a similar patch to the 45° diamond, and the same type of designs can be created in lines as before. However, this diamond can also be stitched into stars and cubes, leading to whole new avenues of creativity.

THE TEMPLATE

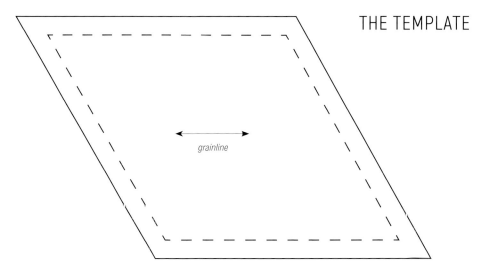

grainline

STITCHING

These diamonds open up a whole new range of design possibilities starting with gentle zigzags and moving on to cubes, hexagons and stars. Use the fabrics to create 3-D effects in your quilt.

Option 1

Option 2

Option 3

DESIGN IDEAS

The pattern in the quilt shown opposite (Design 1) follows an attractive star pattern across the piece.

Design idea 2

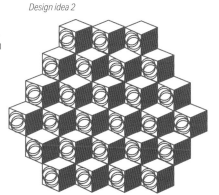

Design idea 3

KITE

This shape will become a firm favourite. The design possibilities open up before you, from triangles to hexagons.

THE TEMPLATE

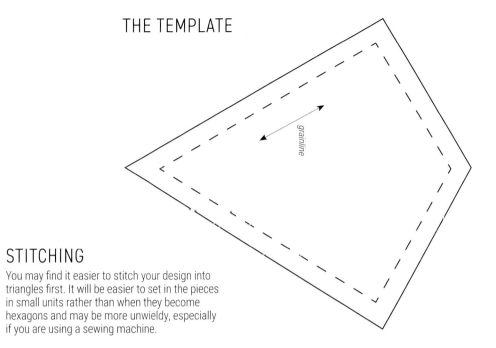

grainline

STITCHING

You may find it easier to stitch your design into triangles first. It will be easier to set in the pieces in small units rather than when they become hexagons and may be more unwieldy, especially if you are using a sewing machine.

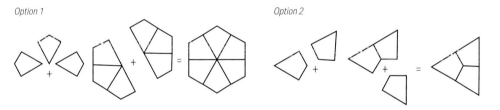

Option 1

Option 2

DESIGN IDEAS

These kites form hexagons in two different fabrics before being sewn together (see Design 1, below).

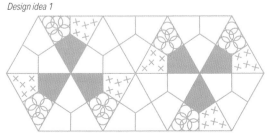

Design idea 1

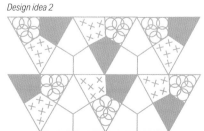

Design idea 2

EQUILATERAL TRIANGLE

This is a lovely shape to play with; easily sewn into larger units such as diamonds, hexagons and larger triangles. On the other hand, it also lends itself beautifully to scrappy charm quilts easily sewn in comfortable rows.

THE TEMPLATE

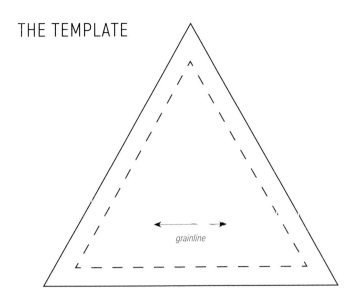

grainline

STITCHING

Depending on your design, work in rows or smaller units before compiling the larger piece.

Option 1

△ + ▽ + △ + ▽ + △ + ▽ + △ + ▽ + △ + ▽

= ◁△▽△▽△▷

Option 2

△ + ▽ + △

▽ + △ + ▽

DESIGN IDEAS

The pattern in the quilt shown opposite (Design 1) creates light and dark diamond shapes.

Design idea 2

Design idea 3

TUMBLER

This long, stretched version of the half-hexagon can give your designs a rather different feel. It's fun to get to grips with the different variations this patch can offer, and it's a great design for using up scrap fabric.

THE TEMPLATE

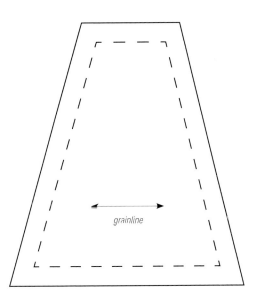

grainline

STITCHING

This patch is easily stitched in rows, omitting any need to set in pieces. You can achieve some very diverse patterns by choosing your fabrics carefully.

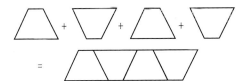

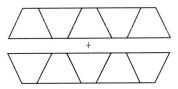

DESIGN IDEAS

Design idea 1

Design idea 2 (as shown opposite)

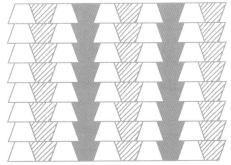

HALF-SQUARE

This is a great little shape that can make so many different quilts. When there is a stark contrast between the two patches in the square, many different combinations can be worked into quite different-looking designs.

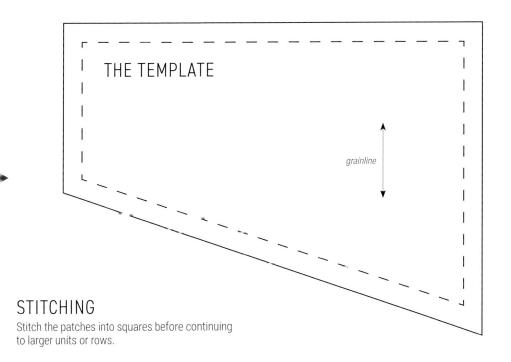

THE TEMPLATE

grainline

STITCHING

Stitch the patches into squares before continuing
to larger units or rows.

Option 1

Option 2

DESIGN IDEAS

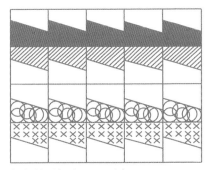

Design idea 1 (as shown opposite)

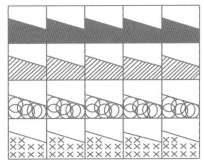

Design idea 2

HALF-HEXAGON

This is a really useful shape to use in your quilts. It allows you to stitch a hexagon quilt without any set-in piecing, as it can all be done in rows. This shape offers so much more, though, and it is well worth delving into your fabric stash to explore the possibilities.

STITCHING

Both options below show you how to work in
rows, removing the need to set in any pieces.

Option 1

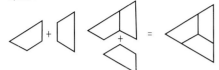

Option 2

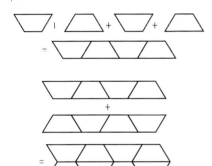

DESIGN IDEAS

The pattern in the quilt shown opposite
(Design 1) creates lovely hexagon shapes.

THE TEMPLATE

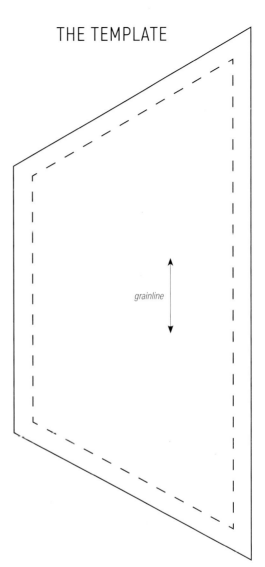

grainline

Design idea 2

Design idea 3

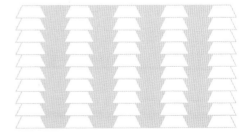

BRAID

It is amazing how one shape can offer so many possible quilts, all of which look so different. Have fun using up your scraps in all the quilt possibilities this patch opens up to you.

STITCHING

The easiest way to stitch linear designs is in lines. This braid design is worked in lines and, once you get started, it all comes together easily.

THE TEMPLATE

Option 1

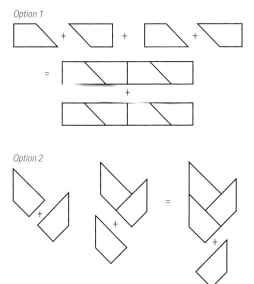

Option 2

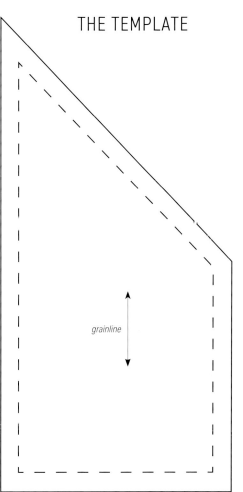

grainline

DESIGN IDEAS

The pattern in the quilt shown opposite (Design 1) creates an attractive red-pink stripy pattern.

Design idea 2

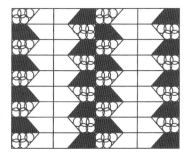

Design idea 3

CLAM SHELL

The question often asked of this pattern is which way up it goes –
ultimately, it is up to the maker. Either way, it is worth having a go at this
classic patch, especially to practise perfecting your curves.

THE TEMPLATE

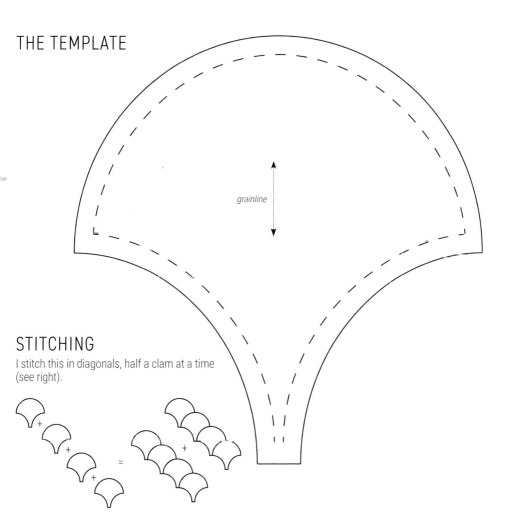

grainline

STITCHING

I stitch this in diagonals, half a clam at a time (see right).

DESIGN IDEAS

The pattern in the quilt shown opposite (Design 1) is completely random, giving it a homemade charm.

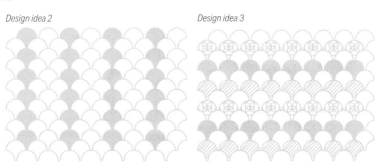

Design idea 2

Design idea 3

HEXAGON

This is the shape most people have in mind when thinking of one patch and tessellating patchwork. Most commonly worked in the EPP method (where you tack/baste around the shape – see page 11), but easily worked in the American piecing method, which cuts out the need to use papers and is then easily transferable to a sewing machine.

THE TEMPLATE

STITCHING

This is often worked in smaller units such as a Grandmother's Flower Garden pattern, then sewn into a larger unit.

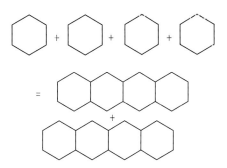

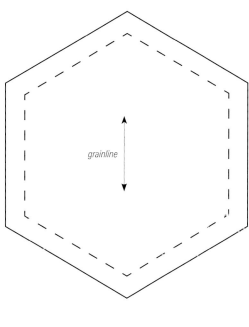

grainline

DESIGN IDEAS

The pattern in the quilt shown opposite (Design 1) is made by creating dark, wavy lines separated by light ones, with a blue and beige theme.

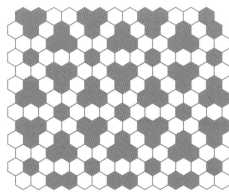

Design idea 2

Design idea 3

JEWEL

Two quite different designs can be made from this patch. Both lend themselves to the use of scraps, but if time and inclination allow, some elaborate overall designs can be produced.

THE TEMPLATE

grainline

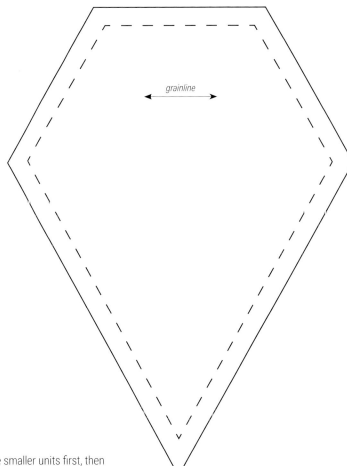

STITCHING

Stitch either design as the smaller units first, then
set them in to each other to create the quilt.

Option 1

Option 2

DESIGN IDEAS

Design idea 1 (as shown below)

Design idea 2

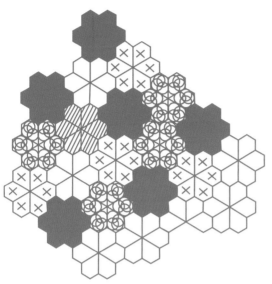

APPLE CORE

A great shape for practising your curved piecing and, once you get the knack, this patch will hold no fear. If it seems a bit daunting, then practise using a larger template before attempting a smaller shape.

THE TEMPLATE

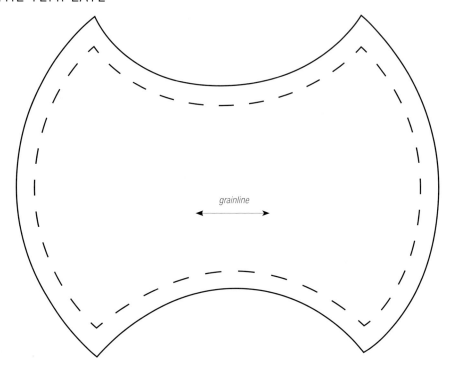

grainline

STITCHING

This is most easily worked in rows, or sew four patches together
to make a square, then work these into rows.

Option 1

Option 2

DESIGN IDEAS

Design idea 1 (as shown below)

Design idea 2

THE QUILT

Whether you want to try out every one-patch block in the book, or just pick a selection of your favourites, this sampler-style quilt with its lovely wide frames is great for showcasing the designs. It's easy to make the quilt as big or as small as you like, and it converts easily to a QAYG project if you want to take it with you on the move.

MEASUREMENTS

Quilt size: 64½ x 64½in (164 x 164cm)

Block size: 12in (30.5cm) finished

Block size with frame/borders: 16in (41cm) finished

FABRIC REQUIREMENTS

- Blocks: 16 blocks sewn from patterns of your choice. I have doubled up on the patterns making two panels from eight designs, but you can use as many or as few as you like. I have placed the blocks so they mirror image each other on the quilt, adding a sense of continuity (see opposite). Make sure that each panel is large enough that you can cut a 12½ x 12½in (32 x 32cm) square from it.

- Frames: one Fat Quarter per block OR 5in (12.75cm) x WOF per block

- Batting/wadding: 74 x 74in (188 x 188cm)

- Backing: 148in (3.8m) x WOF

- Binding: 18in (50cm) x WOF

NOTIONS

- 12½in (32m) square ruler (optional, but helpful)

CUTTING REQUIREMENTS

- 16 blocks, each cut to: 12½ x 12½in (32 x 32cm)

- For frames cut from Fat Quarters:
  - Cut four strips, 2½in (6.5cm) wide
  - Cut two strips, 2½ x 12½in (6.5 x 32cm)
  - Cut two strips, 2½ x 16½in (6.5 x 42cm)

  OR for frames cut from WOF:
  - Cut two strips, 2½in (6.5cm) x WOF
  - From one strip sub-cut two 12½in (32cm) lengths
  - From the other strip sub-cut two 16½in (42cm) lengths

- Backing: cut the fabric into two equal lengths. Remove the selvedge/selvage and join along this edge to make the backing. Press the seam open.

- Binding: cut seven strips of fabric 2½in (6.5cm) wide. Join with bias joins, removing the selvedge/selvage and pressing the seams open. Press in half along the length WS together.

61

INSTRUCTIONS

SEWING THE BLOCKS

1 Cut your panels to 12⅛in (32cm) square. I cut them at the last minute, so that the stitching on the outside edges of the blocks does not start to unravel.

2 Pin the short strips RS together to opposite sides of the panel, aligning the raw edges. Stitch and press the seams towards the frame.

3 Repeat on the remaining two sides of the panel with the long strips.

4 Lay out your framed blocks in to four rows of four blocks. Make sure to alternate the directions of the frames. This way there are no seams to match up when you sew the framed blocks together. Press the seams in each row towards the long (vertical) frames.

5 Now pin the completed rows together. Pin at the junctions of the framed blocks. They will sit snugly together due to the way you have pressed the seams. Sew the rows together, then press these new long seams in one direction.

TACKING/BASTING

6 Once the top is complete, layer and tack/baste with the wadding/batting and backing fabric (see page 12).

QUILTING

7 I quilted with an all-over vermicelli design on a machine to give cohesion to the quilt design. Hand quilting using a design like Amish waves would have the same effect. Or, if you like, you could outline quilt around the shapes in each panel, then around each frame (see page 13).

8 Once you have quilted, remove the tacking/basting and trim the excess wadding/batting and backing.

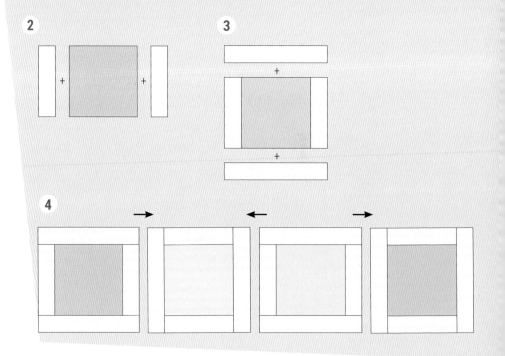

BINDING

9 For this quilt I used hacked mitred corners with a square-corner finish (which results in three mitred corners and one squared).

Start with your binding strip lined up along one edge on the front of the quilt, raw edges matching, and starting from one corner.

Sew the binding along the edge with a ¼in (5mm) seam allowance then stop ¼in (5mm) from the first corner you meet. Fold the binding at a 90-degree angle, away from the quilt and so the free long edge of the binding aligns with the next, unbound edge of the quilt. Fold the binding back down along the next unbound edge, aligning the raw edges and creating a fold at the corner. Start sewing from the folded edge. Sew down to the next corner, and repeat (A).

As you approach the last corner, fold the stitched binding on the first sewn edge away from the quilt, as shown (B).

Lay the rest of the binding along the edge, then stitch right to the edge. Trim off the excess binding (C).

On the back of the quilt and at the square corner, trim away the surplus fabric (and wadding/batting, if necessary) to make the corner less bulky (D).

Turn the binding to the back of the quilt, and cover the raw edges and stitch line of the binding worked from the front of the quilt. Fold and pin the mitred corners; for the square corner, fold and pin as shown, so the corners are 'stepped' (E). Then slip stitch in place at all four corners.

A

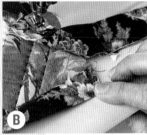

B

C

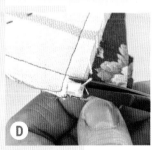

D

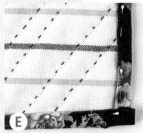

E

ACKNOWLEDGEMENTS

As ever with grateful thanks to the team at Search Press who allow me to continue to spread the word about patchwork and quilting.

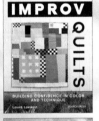